W9-BTO-685

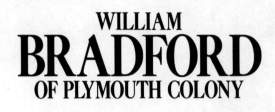

WILLIAM
BRADFORD
OF PLYMOUTH COLONY

WILLIAM
BRADFORD
OF PLYMOUTH COLONY

W. J. Jacobs

A Visual Biography

*Illustrated with authentic prints,
documents, and maps*

Franklin Watts, Inc. / New York / 1974

Historical consultant,
Professor Frederick Kershner, Jr.
Teachers College, Columbia University

Original maps and drawings by William K. Plummer
Photo research by Selma Hamdan
Cover design by Rafael Hernandez

Library of Congress Cataloging in Publication Data

Jacobs, William Jay.
    William Bradford of Plymouth Colony.

    (A Visual biography)
    SUMMARY: A biography of the first governor of the Plymouth Colony who served in that office for thirty years and greatly influenced the development of the community.
    Bibliography: p.
    1. Bradford, William, 1588-1657–Juvenile literature. 2. Massachusetts — History — Colonial period (New Plymouth) — Juvenile literature. [Bradford, William, 1588-1657. 2. Massachusetts — History — Colonial period (New Plymouth)] I. Title.
F68.B8243   974.4'02'0924 [B] [92]   74-870
ISBN 0-531-02724-4

FOR HANNO

A Note on the Illustrations

Many of the illustrations in this book were drawn during the time of the Pilgrims or are photographs of documents or writings of the Pilgrims. These materials give us an idea of how the Pilgrims lived. The drawings of William K. Plummer show the equipment the Pilgrims used in their daily life.

*. . . and as one small candle may light a thousand,
so the light here kindled doth shone to many,
yea in some sorte to our whole nation.*

—*William Bradford*, Of Plimoth Plantation

On November 21, 1620, sixteen armed men boarded a small boat from the *Mayflower*, anchored off the coast of Cape Cod, and rowed to shore. Some of the men were Pilgrims. They had risked their lives in a perilous voyage across the Atlantic Ocean for freedom to practice their religion and, through hard work, to make a reasonable living. Along with the Pilgrims on the *Mayflower* was a somewhat larger group of "Strangers," as the Pilgrims called them — servants, artisans, shopkeepers — recruited by the Merchant Adventurers of London to help make the colony a financial success.

From its small beginnings Plymouth Colony prospered. More important, it became a model in the minds of later Americans. The Pilgrims of Plymouth gave America an example of humane laws that protected personal freedoms. They were responsible for the custom of Thanksgiving Day, with its spirit of gratitude to God for the gifts of life and home and family and food.

Plymouth showed the way, too, in the idea of self-government. In the Mayflower Compact, signed before any colonist set foot on shore, the Pilgrims and their companions agreed to regulate their own affairs and elect their own leaders. In the years that followed, they used the "town meeting" — open to all citizens — to spread the work (and the personal satisfaction) of self-govern-

Tumbril Sledge 1650

ment throughout the society. The men and women of Plymouth were expected not only to do what was good for themselves as individuals but what was good for the community as a whole.

That the Plymouth colony survived at all is probably because of the strength and driving will of one man — William Bradford. An orphan, largely self-educated, he served as governor of the colony for more than thirty years. So completely did he merge his own life with that of the Pilgrim community that it is hard to separate the story of the man, Bradford, from that of his people. Thus Bradford's famous book, *Of Plimoth Plantation*, describes the difficulties and the triumphs of the Pilgrims. (Plimoth is the old way of spelling Plymouth.) But on every page we are able to see, too, the courage, the tenacity, the burning intensity of William Bradford, one of the most engrossing figures in all of America's history.

ENGLAND IN AN
AGE OF TURMOIL

In March, 1590, when William Bradford was born, Queen Elizabeth I of England was in the thirty-second year of her reign. William Shakespeare was beginning to write his plays; Edmund Spenser was writing *The Faerie Queene*, which he dedicated to Elizabeth; Englishmen gathered around blazing logs in the taverns and drank great quantities of spiced ale; and in July, 1588 — less than two years before Bradford's birth — those daring English "sea dogs," Drake, Hawkins, and Grenville, had changed the course of history by driving off the mighty invasion Armada sent by King Philip II of Spain to conquer England.

It was a time of English national greatness — a period of magnificent literature, of expansion and adventure overseas, and of pride in the achievements of a courageous people.

Yet it was also a time of suffering. Men were thrown into prison for small offenses, with little or no chance to prove their innocence. The death penalty was a common punishment, even for minor thefts. Unemployment was high. Many landowners were turning to raising sheep for their wool and needed fewer farmers to care for their pastured sheep. So the highways were filled with thousands of homeless men and women, begging or stealing to stay alive. Disease was common. Enemies of the government were tortured and left to die in prison, or in some cases beheaded, their heads impaled on pikes lining London Bridge.

All of this was part of the tumultuous world into which William Bradford was born. But the age had still another vital ingredient — religion. For many centuries almost all of those people in Western Europe who believed in Christianity had belonged to one Church, the Roman Catholic Church. The common people believed deeply that life on earth was short, a time to be endured before one received either reward in heaven or punishment in hell. Only the Church, they thought, could save men from the horrors of an eternity in hell. People often gave gifts of land and other property to the Church to help assure their salvation (their entry into heaven).

Gradually the Church came to own vast tracts of land across the face of Europe, donated by grateful Christians. The Pope — head of the Church on earth — and his bishops and priests were obeyed by the common people almost without question. The power of the Church was enormous. Meanwhile, church buildings became more ornate, the robes of the priests more costly, Church ceremonies more complicated.

Beginning in about the fourteenth century, Catholic priests and others began to demand reforms — changes — in the Church. One such priest was the Englishman John Wycliffe (c. 1328–1384). But the most important reformer was the German priest Martin Luther (1483–1546).

Luther taught that it was not necessary for people to pray to God through a priest; he said that all of those in a congregation who believed in God were their own priests. (This came to be known as the "priesthood of all believers.") Luther also urged men to pray in their own language, one they understood, not in Latin, as the Roman Catholic Church required. In many countries the

Martin Luther.

Bible was translated into the language of the common people to encourage them to read the Scriptures for themselves and make up their own minds on religious questions.

When Luther was ordered to return to the teachings of the Catholic Church he refused. Instead, he and his followers *protested* against the order and therefore became known as "Protestants." In 1529 Luther formally called for a "reformation" of the Church — simpler services, ministers who would preach sermons based on Bible readings, and a return to the ideas of Jesus Christ himself, as explained in the New Testament.

Other Protestant reformers included John Calvin (1509–1564), a Frenchman living in Geneva, Switzerland, and the Scottish leader John Knox (1505?–1572). In most of the countries of Western Europe Catholics and Protestants fought each other, sometimes in bloody warfare. The major wars of religion lasted until 1648, and in some countries, such as Northern Ireland (Ulster), religious strife continues even to the present day.

In England, King Henry VIII broke with the Catholic Church for reasons of his own and established the Church of England. For a time under Queen Mary (known to history as "Bloody Mary") Catholicism returned to power; Protestants who would not pledge loyalty to the Pope were brutally tortured, burned at the stake, or hung, drawn, and quartered. With the accession to the throne of Queen Elizabeth in 1558 England once again became a Protestant country, and the Catholic citizens were persecuted if they practiced that religion.

But even among English Protestants many crucial religious questions remained unresolved. Some Protestants said that in its ceremonies and beliefs the Church of England was still too much like the Catholic Church; it should be made "purer" — more like Christianity in the time of Jesus. People who believed this came to be called "Puritans."

A cartoon depicting the many-sided dispute over religion in England in the 1600s.

An imaginative engraving of an episode in the wars of religion.

One reformer, Robert Browne, declared that the Church of England would always be "unclean." According to Browne, those who wanted to worship as true Christians should separate entirely from the English Church. Each congregation should elect its own leaders and govern itself, disregarding altogether the rules of the national Church. Leaders in the Church of England thoroughly despised these "Separatists," as Browne's followers were called, and persecuted them even more harshly than Catholics.

Such intense quarrels over religious ideas, so unusual today, were understandable in an age of faith. In the Middle Ages and early modern times people thought as much about the next world — the world after death — as about their earthly lives.

So to young William Bradford and others in the little Yorkshire town of Austerfield, religion was of such importance that in order to worship God as they thought proper they would risk everything, even their lives.

A HAVEN
IN HOLLAND

The town of Austerfield lay in Yorkshire, only about one hundred and fifty miles from London on the Great North Road. But the townspeople knew little of the city's exciting life. They were farmers, making their living from the land and ambitious to own more land. Proud, independent, hardworking, they were part of the so-called yeoman class — the middle class of the time.

The Bradfords were a family of importance in Austerfield, having lived in the area for several generations. Although he was not wealthy and had no title of nobility, William's father (also named William) was prosperous and respected. His mother, Alice Hanson, had been the daughter of the town storekeeper. William was the only son.

In July, 1591, when William was only a year old, his father died. When he was four years old, his mother remarried and sent him to live with his grandfather. Within two years his grandfather died, too. A year later his mother died. William, at the age of seven, was an orphan. He was sent to live with two uncles, Robert and Thomas Bradford. So far, his life had been filled with tragedy and unhappiness.

As a boy, William was delicate and sickly. Possibly because of his weak body, possibly because of his striking intelligence, he was taught to read and write. For a boy in rural England that was somewhat unusual, since at the time large numbers of Englishmen, even in the cities, did not know their letters.

*The church
at Austerfield.*

William took eagerly to reading, treasuring every book he could discover. By the age of twelve he was forming his ideas of the outside world from such advanced sources as *Praise of Folly* (by Erasmus) and drawing his views on religion directly from the Bible. It was an age of intense, exciting religious debate, and in his reading Bradford was especially attracted to religious themes.

Young Bradford somehow began to attend the sermons of the Reverend Richard Clyfton at the neighboring town of Babworth. William's uncles were furious when they found out where he had been, since they were loyal to the Church of England and Clyfton preached the ideas of the Puritans, attacking the national Church. Still, despite their opposition, William stubbornly insisted on walking the sixteen miles to Babworth and back every Sunday.

In 1606 Clyfton became the pastor of a new church located at Scrooby, within easy walking distance of Austerfield. The Scrooby congregation was made up of Separatists — men and women even further from the politically safe views of the Church

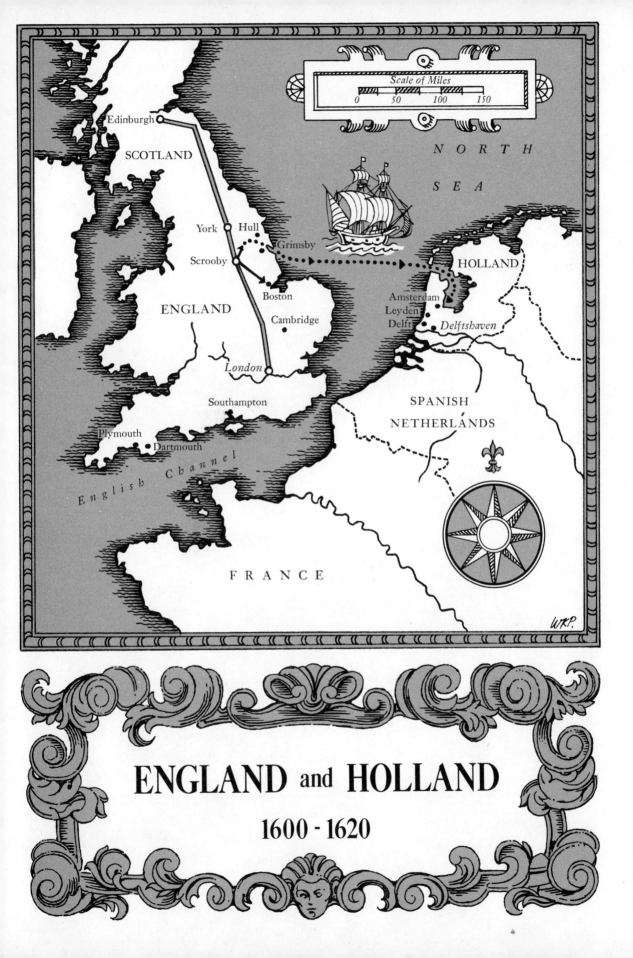

ENGLAND and HOLLAND

1600 - 1620

A view of Scrooby village.

A cartoon satirizing the strictness of a Puritan, who has hung his cat in punishment for killing a mouse on Sunday.

of England. In fact their ideas were so unpopular that they had to meet in direct defiance of the national Church and its leader, the King of England.

In 1603 Queen Elizabeth had died and been succeeded by King James I. James was no friend of the Puritans and Separatists. He clearly understood how dangerous to him it would be, for example, to permit the Separatists to elect their own ministers. If they did, as James put it, it would not be long before "Jack and Tom and Will and Dick shall meete and at their pleasure censure me, and my Councell, and all our proceedinges." By this King James meant that giving people the right to choose their own religious leaders could lead them to demand next the right to choose their own political leaders. For James this was unthinkable, since he believed that kings were placed on their thrones by the will of God. Kings ruled, he said, by "Divine Right." If this were true, then Separatists (like Richard Clyfton and the Scrooby congregation) were enemies of the king and had to be stopped. James ordered an end to private prayer meetings and declared that only the Church of England's prayer book could be used for religious services.

Many Puritans and Separatists refused to obey the orders of King James; they continued to hold prayer meetings, but now in secret, like the early Christians under the rule of the Roman Empire. It was at this time that the congregation at Scrooby was formed, with Richard Clyfton as pastor.

Other important leaders of the church were John Robinson and William Brewster. Brewster, well traveled and politically wise, took a special interest in the sensitive and intelligent seventeen-year-old, William Bradford, who regularly attended the secret meetings of the society. Bradford idolized Brewster, and the sophisticated Brewster treated the promising youth like a son. Stimulated by the attentions of a respected leader more than twice

his age, and no doubt excited by the adventure of belonging to a secret group — in its time a radical group — the orphaned Bradford threw himself into the work of the Separatist community.

Soon, however, the authorities discovered the Scrooby congregation's activities and began to make life in England unbearable for them. Brewster was arrested and fined; other members of the church were threatened. Finally the little band of Separatists could stand no more. As William Bradford later wrote in *Of Plimoth Plantation*, "by a joynte consente they resolved to goe into the Low Countries [the Netherlands], where they heard was freedome of Religion for all men."

Although King James detested the troublesome Separatists and Puritans, he had also decreed that nobody refusing to accept the Church of England could leave the country. The Scrooby congregation tried once to escape by boat, but they were betrayed by a greedy ship's captain and many of their leaders imprisoned. Bradford was one of those made to walk in shame down the main street of Boston, a town in Lincolnshire, with the townspeople lining the roadway. In the spring of 1608, however, most of the congregation succeeded in reaching Amsterdam, Holland, surviving a fearful storm at sea. Within a year the remaining Scrooby Separatists joined the group in Holland and, under the pastorship of John Robinson, some one hundred Pilgrims (as they are known to history) moved to the beautiful Dutch university town of Leyden.

From 1609 to 1620 the Pilgrims lived in Leyden. At first the language and customs were strange to them. Farmers, they had to learn new occupations in a land of trade and manufacturing. Bradford became first a weaver, later a corduroy maker;

William Brewster.

others became carpenters or cobblers or merchants. Eventually they saved enough money to build their own meetinghouse. Every Sunday they met and held services. There were long sermons by the minister, followed by lunch and then a full afternoon of debate and discussion on subjects raised in the Bible.

During their years in Holland the Pilgrims learned much. They became a close-knit community and worked hard at imitating the life of the early Christians — that is, sharing good and bad fortune with each other in brotherhood. In order to survive they were forced to learn useful skills in business and commerce. They also became accustomed to electing their own church leaders and to allowing every man to speak out freely in discussion. All of this would help to prepare them for the great adventure that lay ahead.

For William Bradford the years in Holland were the time of his young manhood, from the age of nineteen to thirty. He became a citizen of Leyden and started his own business. In 1609 he met Dorothy May, then only eleven years old. He waited, and five years later he married her. Most of the inheritance that he received on reaching adulthood went into the house he built for Dorothy; the rest went to the congregation and for tools he needed in business. Soon he and Dorothy had a son, John.

Whatever spare time Bradford had after his church duties he spent reading at Leyden University. There, in the quiet of the library, he educated himself in literature, theology, and ancient languages. Through the years Bradford matured, both as a scholar and as a respected leader of the Pilgrim community. Holland was an important interlude for him.

Leyden, Holland.

Below, Leyden University.

Academia Lugdunensis

Despite the "spirituall comforte" and delights of Leyden, all was not well for the Pilgrims. It was always hard for them to earn a good living in Holland. Poverty was never far away, even after years of effort. More important, the youth of the community, observing the general conduct of Dutch citizens around them, resented having to participate in the Sunday service. To many of them a Pilgrim life seemed too strict to be worthwhile. Some became soldiers or sailors, like their Dutch friends. Others, in Bradford's words, "were drawn away by evill examples into extravagante and dangerous courses." If the children of the Pilgrims were to stray from the group's beliefs, then the community — which was, after all, a *religious* community — would wither away and die.

By 1617 the Pilgrims were beginning to look about for a place where they could live the kind of pure religious life that was difficult to achieve in Holland. It was then that they seriously began to consider moving to the New World — America. There, in the wilderness, they could worship as they chose. There would be fewer of the worldly temptations that surrounded them in Holland. And, like the Old Testament prophets whose example they so often followed, they could own land and return to a life of farming. But the journey to America was dangerous and expensive. How would a small, poor congregation ever achieve so ambitious a goal?

TO THE
PROMISED LAND

The Pilgrims thought first of settling in the British territory of Virginia. But, in answer to their questions about Virginia, King James refused to guarantee them religious freedom. Furthermore, the London Company, which would have had to supply them with ships and supplies, was near bankruptcy.

The Dutch New Netherlands Company offered not only to transport the Pilgrims to Dutch lands on the Hudson River but also to give them free cattle and protect them against the English.

The Pilgrims decided instead to accept the offer of a smooth-talking English iron salesman, Thomas Weston. Weston proposed to form a company that would lend the Pilgrims the money they needed for ships and supplies. After they arrived in America they could pay the money back, with interest. As promised, Weston returned to London and formed a company of seventy Merchant Adventurers who agreed to advance money to the Pilgrims; in return they expected to realize a large profit. Bradford would later remark that the Adventurers were far more concerned with their monetary losses than the loss of life among the settlers, which "cannot be vallewed at any prise."

Through the urging of Sir Ferdinando Gorges it was decided to locate the Pilgrim colony near Cape Cod. There, reasoned the company's backers, the colonists could make a profitable living fishing from the waters off the coast of Massachusetts and Maine.

Fishermen from many European countries already knew that the area swarmed with valuable codfish, easily salted and in great demand in Europe.

The Pilgrims busily prepared for their voyage. Finally, on July 22, 1620, a band of sixteen men, eleven women, and nineteen children embarked from Delftshaven, Holland, for Southampton, England. They sailed on the *Speedwell*, a small ship of about 60 tons. The *Speedwell*, according to plan, was to be the first vessel in the Pilgrims' fishing fleet in America.

Left behind in Holland after a tearful farewell were several members of the Leyden congregation, including some who had chosen not to go and a few of the women and children thought too frail or too young for the arduous journey. Among those left behind was five-year-old John, the son of Dorothy and William Bradford.

At Southampton the Pilgrims were to pick up the remainder of their supplies and to join the *Mayflower*, a ship of 180 tons. Awaiting them, too, were about an equal number of profit-minded "Strangers," as the Pilgrims called them, some with wives and children. The Strangers were tanners, carpenters, barrel makers — workers whom Weston had recruited to swell the ranks of the tiny Pilgrim group and provide practical skills the colony would need, beginning from nothing in the wilderness. There were also some indentured servants, men who in exchange for their passage to America promised to work without pay for seven years. All of the Strangers belonged to the Church of England. Their reasons for going to the New World were largely economic, not religious.

In the purchase of supplies at Southampton there was endless delay and argument. Even more serious, Weston now insisted that the Pilgrims agree to a new condition: that for their first seven years in New England their land, their houses, their profits

— everything — were to be owned and shared equally with the Merchant Adventurers. Contrary to the original contract, they were not even to have two days each week to labor for themselves; all their time was to be spent in work whose results would go partly to the company.

The Pilgrims were dismayed and angry. But with the summer of 1620 passing quickly they had to leave at once or face the perils of an Atlantic crossing and a landing in unknown territory in cold weather. With much grumbling the Pilgrims agreed to Weston's shrewd demands in order to speed their departure. (No contract was signed until 1621, when the Pilgrims, true to their word, went through with the bargain, even though they were already in America.)

On August 5, 1620, the *Mayflower* and the *Speedwell* sailed out of Southampton harbor. Twice, however, they had to return to England because of leaks in the little *Speedwell*. Finally it was decided to abandon the *Speedwell* and to cram everyone together aboard the *Mayflower*. Twenty passengers — perhaps shocked by the crowded conditions — thought better of the expedition and decided to remain in England.

The other one hundred and two colonists squeezed onto the *Mayflower*, a ship only ninety feet long and twenty-six feet wide at its broadest point. The number of passengers was actually twenty-nine over the generous legal limit of the day. For sixty-six days and nights the tiny ship was the home of the brave Pilgrim "Saints" — or believers — as they called themselves, and their comrades in danger, the English Strangers.

Conditions were horrible. There were no toilets, only slush buckets, perhaps concealed behind a curtain. There was scarcely enough water for drinking, none at all for bathing. The food consisted entirely of salt beef or fish, and cold biscuits. The only drink for all, including the company's thirty-three children, was

beer. Beds and hammocks filled almost every inch of space below the top deck, leaving no place for the children to play. The effects of seasickness added to the discomfort and stench in the passengers' compartment. Seawater splashed through cracks in the hull, keeping the settlers' clothing and blankets wet and soggy through the entire voyage. There was virtually no privacy, no opportunity to laugh or cry without sharing the emotion among the entire company. During the ocean passage one man died and one baby, aptly named Oceanus, was born.

Storms, stirring fierce winds and high seas, moved the devout Pilgrim Saints to sing aloud biblical Psalms for hours at a time. This in turn gave rise to shouts and jeers from some of the Strangers. As Anglicans (members of the Church of England), they feared that God might be angered by the sinful beliefs of the Separatists and sink the ship, taking the faithful to a watery grave along with the unfaithful. Unperturbed by criticism, the Pilgrims continued to sing.

At last, on November 20, 1620, the *Mayflower* pulled within sight of land. It was Cape Cod. In his usual understated way Bradford writes that the colonists were "not a little joyful."

Mingled soon with their happiness, however, were unmistakable signs of danger. The *Mayflower* still rode at anchor in what is today Provincetown harbor; not a passenger had stepped ashore. Suddenly several of the colonists excitedly pointed out that Virginia, not New England, was listed in the official patent as the destination of the *Mayflower*.

If the colonists really were outside of the land grant legally reserved for them there could be trouble. It would not even be certain that they had to obey English laws or the commands of

The Mayflower *under sail.*

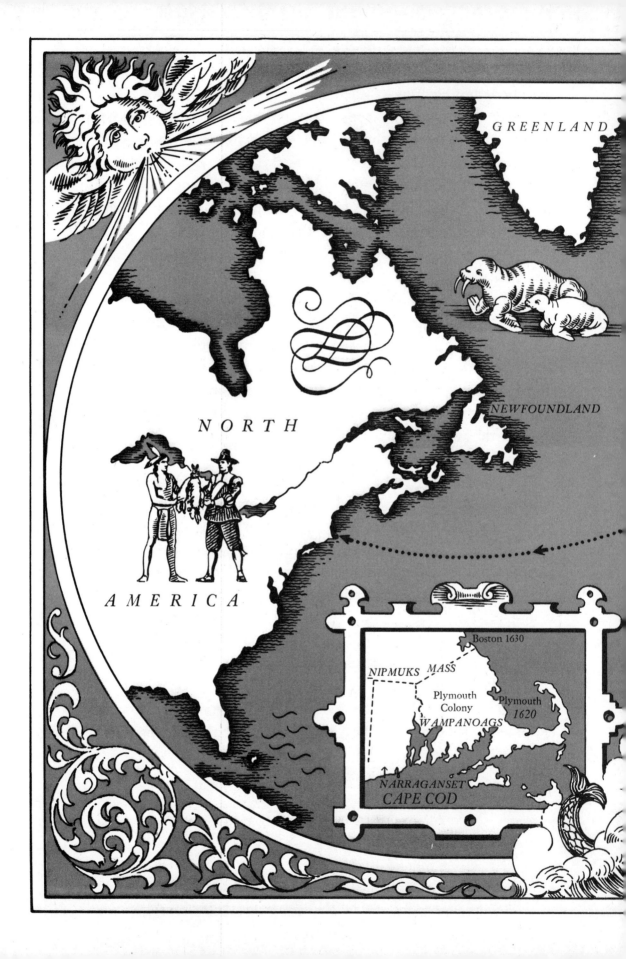

GREENLAND

NEWFOUNDLAND

N O R T H

A M E R I C A

Boston 1630

NIPMUKS MASS

Plymouth
Colony
WAMPANOAGS

Plymouth
1620

NARRAGANSET
CAPE COD

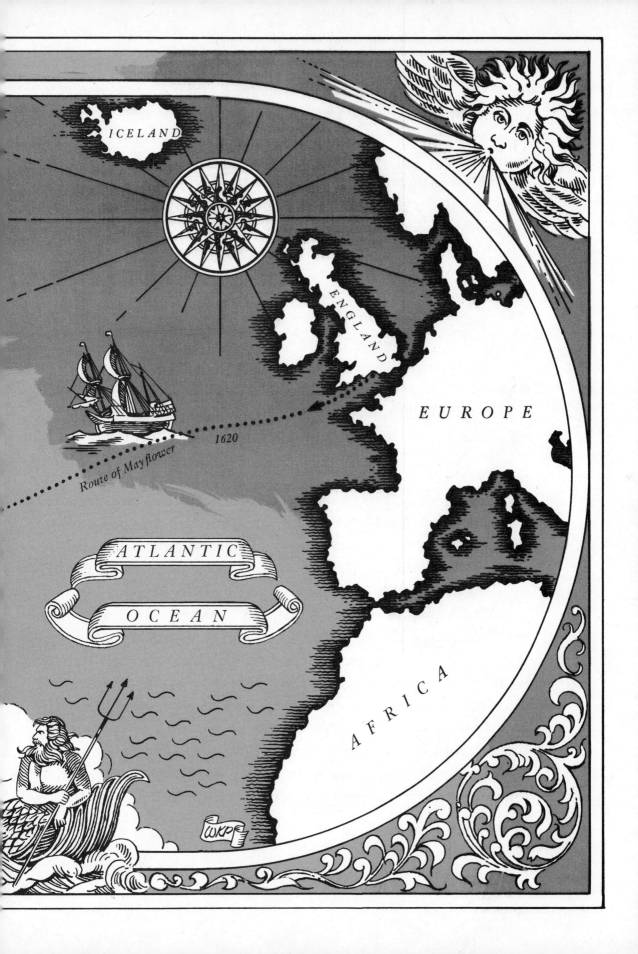

ICELAND

ENGLAND

EUROPE

Route of Mayflower

1620

ATLANTIC

OCEAN

AFRICA

WKP

their own leaders. Ashore, in a wilderness continent, the result could be the rule of force and violence. Nearly two thirds of the colonists were not Separatists but Strangers, mostly poor — with nothing to lose. Such a group might prove hard to handle.

Many historians today argue that the "Northern Virginia" spoken of in the patent legally included New England, and that the Pilgrim leaders intended all along to plant their colony near Cape Cod. But in the tense hours after land was first sighted there was confusion, shouting — and an open threat of mutiny aboard the *Mayflower*.

Acting quickly, the Pilgrim leaders drew up an agreement that has become known to history as the Mayflower Compact. Probably it was written by William Brewster, the religious leader of the colony. But undoubtedly such important men as John Carver and William Bradford had a share in editing and modifying it.

In the Mayflower Compact the Pilgrims agreed to organize the colony into a "civill body politik" — to join together in forming a government. They would make their own laws, elect their own officers. Although women and the men without property (servants) were not to share equally in governing the colony, all freemen aboard the *Mayflower* would. (Freemen were those who were independent citizens, not owing a term of service to anyone.)

The Mayflower Compact is a remarkable document, one of the cornerstones of the American tradition. It provided for government by consent (agreement) of the governed — an idea that would become an accepted part of life in most of the American colonies and a vital point in America's Declaration of Independence from Great Britain. No colonial people had ever dared to establish their own free government. But for the Pilgrims it was not an unusual thing to do; their church organization provided for an elected minister and democratic debate. In a moment of

A facsimile of
the Mayflower Compact.

crisis they merely carried democratic church practices over into the world of politics.

If the Strangers had refused to accept the compact, it never could have worked. But one by one they stepped to the table in the great cabin of the *Mayflower* and signed the document. Probably the first Stranger to sign was the dashing Captain Miles Standish, a soldier hired by the Merchant Adventurers to teach the colonists to defend themselves. For many years his influence with the Strangers and loyalty to Bradford were important to the colony. Even many of the servants signed the compact, promising to live by the rules of the group.

After the signing, John Carver of the Leyden community

was elected governor of the colony — not appointed by the king of England but freely elected by the people.

It was too late on that historic day, November 21, 1620, for the Pilgrims to do much more than row ashore, look around, and return to the *Mayflower*. The next day, Sunday, was set aside for prayer. Then on Monday, November 23, the women were rowed to the beach. Their job was to wash the mountain of dirty clothing heaped up during the long ocean voyage of more than two months. With that simple but necessary task began the daily life of the Pilgrims in America.

"HARD AND
DIFFICULTE BEGINNINGS"

For many months before the departure from England William Bradford had been intensely occupied. In Leyden he had helped to sell the property of the Pilgrims in order to buy supplies. At Southampton he had tried unsuccessfully to hold Weston to the terms of the original contract — and had argued against the less favorable, perhaps even unfair new conditions. Aboard the *Mayflower*, as a leader of the Leyden group (and as a man who liked to work through compromise) he must have been one of those most active in trying to prevent conflict between Saints and Strangers. He was a signer of the Mayflower Compact. Then on November 25 and 26, he was one of the exploring party that considered possible sites for the colony, finally settling upon Plymouth. Legend has it that members of the exploring party stepped to shore from a large rock, preserved today as "Plymouth Rock."

Bradford returned to the *Mayflower* to shattering news. Dorothy, his wife, was dead at the age of twenty-two — drowned in the calm waters where the ship lay anchored. Whether she fell overboard or jumped is a mystery that probably will remain unsolved. Bradford's entry in his journal reads simply, "William Bradford his wife died soon after their arrival."

After Dorothy's death Bradford became even more absorbed in his work. He threw himself into planning and building at the site of Plymouth. Cottages and a "common house" (for storage and meetings) were constructed in the English style, with thatched

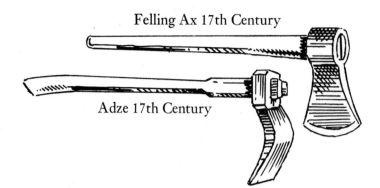

Felling Ax 17th Century

Adze 17th Century

roofs. But before the buildings could be fully completed sickness struck the colony.

The disease — perhaps tuberculosis or pneumonia — spread quickly. Sometimes two or three colonists died in a single day. Often there were only six or seven persons well enough to tend the sick and bury the dead. Even Bradford, strong and hearty as an adult, fell ill, but he recovered. Many children were victims of the disease; whole families died out.

By the end of April only eleven of the twenty-four heads of family survived. Only four of the married women and six of the twenty-nine bachelors (including servants and hired workers) still lived.

Just then, with the colony at its lowest strength, a tall, handsome Indian warrior walked boldly into Plymouth settlement and addressed the startled settlers in English.

"Welcome," he said. "I am Samoset."

Samoset told the colonists that he had learned English while sailing on British ships along the Atlantic coast. He explained that Plymouth stood on the former site of an Indian village, Patuxet. In 1617 all the Indians living there had died of a disease, probably smallpox brought by white merchants.

Samoset stayed overnight at Plymouth. Two days later he returned to the colony with five more warriors and valuable beaver skins to trade. Within a few days Samoset returned again to Plymouth. This time he brought with him Massasoit, the powerful chief of the Wampanoag, who lived at nearby Sowams on Narragansett Bay. Also present was another Indian, named Squanto.

Surprisingly, Squanto spoke even more perfect English than Samoset. He had been in Europe, carried there by an exploring party headed by the English sea captain George Weymouth. Years later he had been reunited with his family, probably by

Indians of the northeastern coast, from a map drawn in the 1600s.

Captain John Smith, hero of the Jamestown, Virginia, colony, only to be sold into slavery in Spain by another Englishman. Converted to Catholicism, he somehow managed to escape to England. Then he returned to New England in a trading vessel. Home at last, he discovered to his horror that the entire village of Patuxet had been wiped out by disease (just as Samoset had explained). Chief Massasoit had then taken in the unhappy Squanto to live among the Wampanoag.

Chief Massasoit was pleased to see the white men. He hoped for their help against a neighboring tribe. The Pilgrims, for their part, were eager to stay at peace with Massasoit's people. The result was a treaty of peace and friendship, one that both sides honored until after Massasoit's death in 1661.

After the treaty was signed, the Indians departed, except for Squanto, who stayed on to live at Plymouth. In the days and weeks that followed his advice made the difference between life and death for the settlers. He taught them to plant Indian corn and other crops, to catch fish both for food and fertilizer, to use maple syrup, to trap deer, and, if they wished, to follow the rivers inland for beaver. Squanto became William Bradford's special friend, his translator, and his most important aide in dealing with other Indian tribes. Bradford described Squanto's coming as nothing less than "another providence of God." Here was further proof, he suggested, of God's special concern for the Pilgrims.

In that same April of 1621, Governor John Carver died. William Bradford, trusted for his good judgment, energy, and strength of will, was elected to replace Carver as leader of the colony. He was thirty-one years old. At that time supplies were running low; there would be no harvest until autumn; and the *Mayflower* had returned to England. It was a serious situation. Still, the winter's trials were over, and Plymouth Plantation had survived. The settlers were of good hope.

Clam Rake

*An Indian of the Northeast,
drawn by John White.*

Wooden Spade

Autumn brought a glorious harvest. Game was plentiful. Trade with the Indians had filled the storehouse with beaver skins. In gratitude the Pilgrims agreed to set aside a day of Thanksgiving.

Through several frantic days the Plymouth settlers prepared for the great feast. Unlike today's celebration, the first Thanksgiving probably took place in the warm October sunshine. The food was bounteous. There were ducks and geese and wild turkeys, lobster, clams, mussels, and eels, fruits and berries, corn bread, and the finest red and white wines the Pilgrims' vineyards could produce. Massasoit and ninety Wampanoag warriors responded to Governor Bradford's invitation to the festival, bearing with them as their share of food five freshly killed deer.

For three days white men and red men played games of strength together. They ate and drank. And, as no occasion could be all play for the serious, hardworking Plymouth Saints, the Pilgrims gave thanks to God for standing by them during their time of trouble. The gifts of life, food, and family, along with the friendship of their neighbors, had deep meaning for men and women who had suffered much.

Fish Cleaning

THE GOVERNORSHIP OF
WILLIAM BRADFORD

Even before the Pilgrims had arrived in America, William Bradford had been a leader in the community of Saints. But Bradford's greatest contributions to his people came as governor of Plymouth colony. He was perfectly suited to the needs of leadership in a wilderness country — a man of ability, confident in his judgment of what needed to be done and in his capacity to do it.

Thoughtful and unhurried, a serious scholar, Bradford could also be firm. Once, when a raid of unfriendly Indians seemed likely, he ordered everyone to work on the completion of a fortification, even though it was Christmas Day. Some of the Strangers refused, saying it was against their conscience. Bradford walked away. Returning later, he found the men playing at sports, such as "stoole ball," in the street. Angrily he stopped the games and took away the players' equipment, declaring that it was against *his* conscience for them to play while their companions worked. Bradford applied his high standard of justice and fair play equally to all at Plymouth Plantation. Otherwise it is doubtful that his strong-minded followers would have been satisfied to elect him governor more than thirty times, insisting that he serve long after he pleaded to be relieved of his duties.

Bradford was a different kind of public official than the settlers had known in Europe. As chief judge of the colony he held the power of life and death over every citizen. Yet he did not abuse his power. Moreover, every day he worked in his shirt-

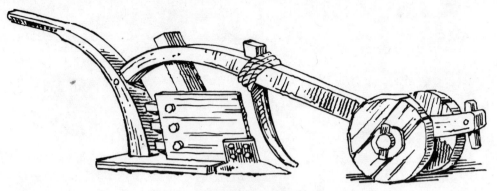
One-handled Plow 17th Century

sleeves alongside the others in the field, planting and harvesting, nailing shingles onto the houses — sweating like everyone else to wrench a living from the American fields and forests. Whatever he achieved in life came from his own labor, not the work of a subject people.

But if Bradford was a "self-made man," he always understood the contributions of others to Plymouth's survival. There was William Brewster, the colony's leader in religious matters, one who had been almost a father to the orphaned Bradford in Scrooby and Leyden; Miles Standish, the short, red-haired soldier, courageous if short-tempered — a man willing to kill if necessary to defend Bradford's community of peaceful Saints; Edward Winslow, the extraordinary ambassador equally at home in a forest encampment of Indians or the elegant court of British kings; John Alden, like Standish a Stranger, brought on the *Mayflower* for his skill as a barrel maker but later taken into the inner circle of Bradford's confidence for his dependability, steadiness, and balanced judgment. (Young John Alden's courtship of Priscilla Mullins at Plymouth was later immortalized in a popular poem by Henry Wadsworth Longfellow.) These unusual men helped Bradford to build a society in the wilderness, where previous rank meant nothing — and only ability counted.

THE BIBLE
AND
HOLY SCRIPTVRES
CONTEYNED IN
THE OLDE AND NEWE
Testament.

TRANSLATED ACCOR-
ding to the Ebrue and Greke, and conferred With
the best translations in diuers langages.

WITH MOSTE PROFITABLE ANNOTA-
tions vpon all the hard places, and other things of great
importance as may appeare in the Epistle to the Reader.

FEARE YE NOT, STAND STIL, AND BEHOLDE
the saluacion of the Lord, which he wil shewe to you this day. Exod. 14.13.

THE LORD SHAL FIGHT FOR YOU: THEREFORE
holde you your peace. Exod. 14. verse 14.

AT GENEVA.
PRINTED BY ROVLAND HALL
M.D.LX.

Sith Hook 1650

The Pilgrims placed their real trust, however, less in men than in God. At one time they had suffered a series of serious misfortunes. Supplies of food were almost exhausted. A summer drought parched the land. The colonists, their clothing in tatters, were in desperate straits. As a last resort Bradford declared a day of fasting and prayer; the settlers were to humble themselves before God. In solemn procession the bedraggled Pilgrims marched up the hill overlooking the sea, where their fortress was located. Bradford, wearing his long judge's robe, walked at the rear, with Brewster and Standish at his side. All day long they prayed. By morning a "soft, sweet raine" began to fall. It continued for fourteen days, saving the colony's crop of corn. To Bradford, it was clearly the work of God.

In the summer of 1622 William Bradford learned that Alice Southworth of London had become a widow. When both were members of the church at Leyden he had known and respected her. Now, at the age of thirty-two, Bradford hoped for her companionship. He wrote to Alice, asking if she would come to Plymouth to be his bride. To his delight, she agreed. On August 24, 1623, they walked together up the path to Fort Hill, the town fortress, where they were married. It was a civil marriage, since the Pilgrims always strictly separated church and state (religious matters and legal matters).

Eventually William and Alice Bradford produced three children of their own — William, Mercy, and Joseph. John Brad-

A deed signed by John Alden,
dated July 20, 1653.

Below, a copy of the "Geneva" Bible,
the version of the Bible that the
Pilgrims brought with them to America.

ford, William's son by Dorothy May, came to live in America when he was twelve, after seven years of separation from his father. Alice's two sons by her previous marriage, Constant and Thomas Southworth, were also part of the expanding household, as was Nathaniel Morton, the son of Alice's sister. Governor Bradford also took into his home four orphan boys, one of whom, Thomas Cushman, he adopted as his own son. Somehow Bradford managed to fit all of the young people into his modest home and to arrange for their education. (He regretted never being able to persuade the citizens of Plymouth to establish free public schools.)

Bradford's sons by Alice, the two Southworth boys, and the brilliant Thomas Cushman all became leaders in the life of the colony, Cushman serving as ruling elder from 1649 until his death in 1691. John, Bradford's son by Dorothy May, later married, moved to nearby Duxbury, and then to Norwich, Connecticut. His life was generally undistinguished and he left no children. Bradford's descendents from his marriage to Alice Southworth, however, today number several thousand persons, including such figures as Robert Bradford, governor of Massachusetts in the 1940s.

The presence of women and children in his household must have made William Bradford even more keenly aware of the need for a strong military defense. The Pilgrims saw the Indians surrounding them in the forest as the greatest threat to their safety. In dealing with the Indians Bradford tried to combine kindness with firmness. Bradford was especially kind in his relations with

An engraving showing agricultural work of northeastern Indians.

the people of Squanto and Massasoit. The Pilgrims nursed the Indians when they were ill, once even saving Massasoit's life.

But when it was necessary, Bradford could be as hard as Plymouth Rock. On one occasion the Narragansetts boldly challenged Plymouth, delivering to the settlement a bundle of arrows tied with a snakeskin. Bradford knew that he could show no sign of weakness. He filled the snakeskin with bullets and returned it to the Indians with a message: the Pilgrims, he said, had not hurt the Narragansett people; they wanted peace, not war; but they were not afraid, and if the Indians desired battle, they should come ahead; Plymouth was ready for them. The Narragansetts backed down.

There was a lesson for the Pilgrims in the crisis — always to be prepared. In preparation for a possible attack Bradford and Standish led the townspeople in working night and day until they had built a palisaded wall, eleven feet high and one mile long, completely encircling their homes and Fort Hill. Guards were posted and fire-fighting teams organized. Cannon were made ready. Fortunately the Pilgrims were never called upon to test the defenses of their community.

On two occasions the Pilgrims took the offensive against the Indians. In March, 1622, Bradford sent Miles Standish and eight men against Chief Wituwamat and his Massachusetts Indian braves, who gave the appearance, to the settlers at least, of threatening Plymouth. Miles Standish and his men trapped Wituwamat. They killed him and three of his warriors. Then they returned to Plymouth carrying the chief's head, which they mounted on a pike atop the highest point of the fort. This was the normal practice following the execution of traitors at that time in Europe. Pastor John Robinson of Leyden, learning about the incident, wrote to Bradford: "Oh! how happy a thing had it been, if you had converted some, before you had killed any." For Bradford

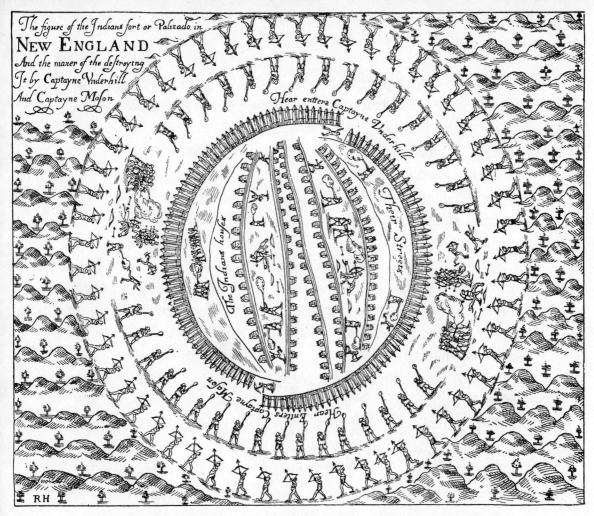

An engraving showing the colonists' attack on the Pequot Indian fort.

to allow such behavior was perhaps uncharacteristic of him. Yet in defending the colony against the menace of Indians he always acted with great vigor. He reasoned that the very survival of Plymouth Plantation was at stake. It should be remembered, too, that men of the time tended to think of Indians as savages, certainly less human than white men.

In 1637 Plymouth reluctantly agreed to join with the colonies of Massachusetts Bay and Connecticut in a war of extermination against the Pequot Indians. Within three weeks some seven hundred Pequot men, women, and children were killed — many of them burned alive — and the survivors sold into slavery.

Then, in 1643, Plymouth joined with Massachusetts Bay, Connecticut (Hartford and surrounding towns), and New Haven to form the New England Confederation. The member colonies had grown alarmed at the increase of hit-and-run attacks by the restless Narragansetts, fearing that open warfare might begin. The English colonists pledged to help each other if attacked by the Indians, or by the French settlements in Canada, or the Dutch in New Netherlands. Seeing the unity of the English, the Narragansetts gave up any plans they might have had for war. Later, under the urging of Bradford, the New England Confederation made a few, largely unsuccessful attempts to Christianize the Indians. As Pastor Robinson feared, the English were far more active in killing the Indians of the Northeast than in converting them.

In King Philip's War (1675–76), the last major Indian resistance in New England was ruthlessly crushed, some of the white soldiers appearing to take great pleasure in their work. But this was well after Bradford's death.

Along with matters of defense, much of Bradford's time as governor went into managing the colony's business. One of the first important decisions he made was to end Plymouth's experiment with a communal economy. According to the settlers' agreement with the Merchant Adventurers there was to be a division of profits at the end of seven years. Until then the colonists could own no personal property. No matter how hard a man worked, he got just as much to eat, just as nice a house as the man who did nothing. By 1623 the colony was on the brink of starvation.

Bradford took decisive action. He announced that each man would raise his own food, each family would take care of its own plot of land and its own home. Whether for good or evil, said Bradford, it was only human nature for men to want more for themselves and their families. As leader of the colony Bradford had personally broken the contract with the Merchant Adven-

A Samp Mortar

A facsimile of the Plymouth settlement in 1622, showing Governor Bradford's house in the lower right.

turers; and he took full responsibility for doing it. Soon, however, he was able to report with satisfaction how much harder the settlers were working when the profits were at least partially their own.

In 1626 the Pilgrims bought all rights to the colony from the Merchant Adventurers. The price, £1,800, was high. And as Bradford noted, going further into debt was risky. The debt, in fact, was not fully paid until 1648. But meanwhile the Pilgrims were free of the profit-hungry Adventurers.

To win the support of the Strangers Bradford further arranged in 1627 to complete the task of dividing the colony's property — land, houses, and cattle — among the settlers. Virtually every man at Plymouth had a share in the division.

Because Bradford and the officers of the colony undertook to pay the £1,800 debt themselves, they were given a monopoly of the colony's trade. There was some jealousy over their monopoly. Also, in 1639 a complaint arose among the Strangers. They claimed that since 1630 land grants to the people had stopped. In that year the Council for New England (established by the king) had given Bradford, in the so-called Warwick patent, certain special privileges for his rule in Plymouth, including land titles. The Strangers charged that Bradford was keeping all of the land for himself.

On March 15, 1639, the colonists jammed noisily into the meeting room of the fort for a session of the General Court — much like the annual New England town meetings. As Bradford rose to speak the crowd fell silent. The governor reviewed all that had happened since the landing of the *Mayflower*, the sacrifices made by both Saints and Strangers. Then, dramatically, Bradford offered, on behalf of himself and the colony's other officials, to divide among the freemen of Plymouth any lands that were his by the Warwick patent, except for a few tracts. In so doing Bradford gave up much of the land that is present-day Cape Cod. But he kept the colony from splintering in jealous conflict.

The Pilgrims had other problems relating to money. Once, Bradford's trusted deputy, Isaac Allerton, was serving as Plymouth's agent in England. There he diverted several thousand pounds of the colony's money to buy goods that he hoped to sell for his own profit. He also built up huge debts for the colony in wild schemes, spending, for example, £113 on salt because it was a bargain. To Bradford and the Pilgrim elders it seemed unbelievable that a respected member of the church, a man personally sworn to obey specific instructions on his mission, would break his solemn oath and betray his own comrades. But that is precisely what happened. It took many years for the colony to make up for Allerton's treachery.

Another time it was discovered that Thomas Morton, a renegade English lawyer, was trading guns, ammunition, and liquor to the Indians. He was using the trading post at Mount Wollaston originally started by Thomas Weston. (This was the same Thomas Weston who had taken advantage of the Pilgrims in arranging their trip to America. Later he had come to the New World, hoping to become wealthy trading with the Indians.) Bradford referred to Thomas Morton's trading post as "Merry Mount" because, he said, the white traders there had "set up a May-pole, drinking and dancing about it many days together, inviting the Indean women . . . dancing and frisking together."

The Pilgrims were no strangers to strong drink; they enjoyed alcohol. Nor were they prudish about sex. But they could not tolerate white men supplying firearms and liquor to the Indians. It is also possible that they were displeased at the competition of Morton's trading post with their own fur trading ventures. Finally, the Pilgrims, deeply religious, could not help being offended by what they doubtless viewed as heathen festivals and customs, including the hated Maypole. Hostile to paganism and fearful of its influence on their own youth, the Pilgrims grew increasingly uneasy about their frolicsome neighbors.

In any event, after Morton refused to heed Bradford's warning to stop trading in munitions and firewater, the governor sent Miles Standish and a small group of armed men to "Merry Mount." The Pilgrims routed the post's drunken defenders, captured Thomas Morton, and cut down the Maypole. Later they hoisted Morton aboard a ship with block and tackle and shipped him back to England.

One problem that Bradford could never solve was the growth of a powerful neighbor to the north — the Massachusetts Bay Colony. The leaders of the Bay Colony were Englishmen of property and influence: John Winthrop, John Cotton, Sir Richard Saltonstall, John Endicott. They came with supplies, tools, weapons, and, even as early as 1630, far more settlers than Plymouth ever had. (By 1644 the population of Plymouth was 3,000, that of the Bay Colony 15,000.) In religion the citizens of Massachusetts Bay were Puritans, so William Bradford had no difficulty striking up a continuing friendship with John Winthrop, the great Bay Colony leader. And the two communities worked together in defense against the Indians. Massachusetts Bay, however, was less democratic in government than Plymouth, more rigid both in religion and in granting rights to its settlers. It was the Puritans of Boston, not the Pilgrims of Plymouth, who cruelly persecuted Quakers and hanged persons accused of practicing witchcraft.

In 1691 the mighty Massachusetts Bay Colony absorbed Plymouth. But by then William Bradford no longer was alive to protect his community of Saints and Strangers.

THE LEGACY OF
WILLIAM BRADFORD AND
PLYMOUTH COLONY

William Bradford began writing his important history, *Of Plimoth Plantation*, in 1630, when he was forty years old. In less than two years he had completed the story of the Pilgrims to their landing in America. By 1650 he had stopped writing. His faith in the great mission of Plymouth colony still burned brightly, but much had changed. William Brewster, his dearest friend, was dead. Edward Winslow had returned to England to live out his remaining years. Miles Standish had grown old and tired. Meanwhile, many of the Plymouth families, seeking better farmland, had moved out to nearby locations — Duxbury, Scituate, Barnstable, Yarmouth, Taunton. Bradford saw that with prosperity the old closeness, the cement that bound the Pilgrim community together, was disintegrating. And if this was true, then the government and the church of Plymouth could not long survive. It seemed to Bradford that his life's work was crumbling before his eyes.

Discouraged, he nevertheless worked on. He read the classic Greek and Latin writers. He began, in his sixties, to write poetry. He tried to improve his knowledge of Hebrew, hoping to come closer to understanding the Old Testament prophets whom the Pilgrims so admired. He enjoyed the happy company of his many grandchildren swarming playfully around him. And he watched with pride the successes of his sons in the government of the colony. Occasionally he put on his red waistcoat with silver but-

And first of ye occasion, and Endusments ther vnto; the which
that I may truly vnfould, I must begine at ye very roote & rise
of ye same The which I shall endeuor to manefest in a plaine
stile; with singuler regard vnto ye simple trueth in all things,
at least as near as my slender Judgmente can attaine
the same

1 Chapter

It is well knowne vnto ye godly, and judicious, how euer since ye
first breaking out of ye lighte of ye gospell, in our Honourable nation of England (which was ye first of nations, whom ye Lord adorn-
ed ther with, after ye grosse darknes of popery which had couer-
ed, & ouerspred ye christian world) what warrs, & oppositions euer
since satan hath raised, maintained, and continued against the
saincts, from time, to time, in one sorte, or other. Some times by
bloody death & cruell torments, other whiles Imprisonments, banish-
ments, & other hard vsages As being loath his kingdom should goe
downe, the trueth preuaile; and ye churches of god reuerte to their
anciente puritie, and recouer, their primatiue order, libertie, &
bewtie But when he could not preuaile by these means, against
the maine trueths of ye gospell, but that they began to take rooting
in many places; being watered with ye blooud of ye martires,
and blesed from heauen with a gracious encrease He then begane to take him to his anciente strategemes, vsed of old against
the first christians That when by ye bloody, & barbarous per-
secutions of ye Heathen Emperours, he could not stoppe, & subuerte
the course of ye gospell; but that it speedily ouerspred, with
a wounderfull celeritie, the then best known parts of ye world
. He then begane to sow errours, heresies, and wounderfull
disentions amongst ye professours them selues (working vpon their
pride, & ambition, with other corrupte pasions, Incidente to
all mortall men; yea to ye saints them selues in some measure)
By which wofull effects followed; as not only bitter contentions, &
hartburnings, schismes, with other horrible confusions But
satan tooke occasion & aduantage therby to foyst in a number
of vile coremoneys, with many vnprofitable Cannons, & decrees
which haue since been as snares, to many poore, & peacable
souls, euen to this day So as in ye anciente times, the persecuti-

tons, his gay colored hat, or his Turkey grogram suit. His wealth, mostly in land, increased until he was probably the wealthiest man at Plymouth.

But what William Bradford desired most did not happen. Plymouth did not remain, as in the days of its greatest hardships, a community united in the worship of God. Since the days of Scrooby and Leyden Bradford had dreamed of a small, manageable community where all men would be brothers in religion and in the happiness they received from sacrifice to the common good. But both he and the other Pilgrims had learned the difficulty of walking the narrow tightrope between godliness and worldliness, between faith and profit.

Yet even if Bradford's dream of a lasting "community spirit" was never entirely realized, America still owes much to the example of the Pilgrims and Plymouth: fair laws, combining justice for the accused with safety for the community; the Mayflower Compact, a model of how free people can set the rules for their own governance; Thanksgiving Day, an American holiday that celebrates the joys of prosperity while reminding men that life and health and home and family are gifts not entirely of their own making.

On May 17, 1657, William Bradford took to his bed. Two days later he made his will. That evening, with his wife, Alice, at his side, he died. He was buried atop the hill he had climbed so many times, overlooking the Atlantic and his beloved Plymouth colony.

*A facsimile of the
first page of William Bradford's*
Of Plimoth Plantation.

A NOTE ON SOURCES

A necessary starting point for any investigation of Bradford is his own magnificent work, *Of Plimoth Plantation*. See the edition by Samuel Eliot Morison (Knopf, 1952). Of the secondary works the most valuable are *Saints and Strangers*, by George F. Willison (Reynal and Hitchcock, 1945), and Bradford Smith's *Bradford of Plymouth* (Lippincott, 1951). The literature on the Pilgrims and Plymouth is, of course, very extensive.

INDEX

THE AUTHOR

William Jay Jacobs, who has taught at Rutgers and Harvard universities and at Hunter College, is now Distinguished Visiting Professor at Ramapo College of New Jersey. He is the author of a new American history textbook, as well as the Visual Biographies of *Prince Henry the Navigator*, *Hernando Cortes*, and *Samuel de Champlain*.